Information in War: Its Acquisition and Transmission, Part 2

George Armand Furse

The BiblioGov Project is an effort to expand awareness of the public documents and records of the U.S. Government via print publications. In broadening the public understanding of government and its work, an enlightened democracy can grow and prosper. Ranging from historic Congressional Bills to the most recent Budget of the United States Government, the BiblioGov Project spans a wealth of government information. These works are now made available through an environmentally friendly, print-on-demand basis, using only what is necessary to meet the required demands of an interested public. We invite you to learn of the records of the U.S. Government, heightening the knowledge and debate that can lead from such publications.

Included are the following Collections:

- Budget of The United States Government
- Presidential Documents
- United States Code
- Education Reports from ERIC
- GAO Reports
- History of Bills
- House Rules and Manual
- Public and Private Laws
- Code of Federal Regulations
- Congressional Documents
- Economic Indicators
- Federal Register
- Government Manuals
- House Journal
- Privacy act Issuances
- Statutes at Large

CHAPTER IV.

CAVALRY COVERING THE FRONT OF AN ARMY.

NOTWITHSTANDING that the destroying effect of modern firearms has to a certain extent curtailed the action of cavalry on the battle-field, the services which that arm can render in war continue to be of the highest value. Amongst these, covering an army in the field, exploring and feeling for the enemy, can be justly reckoned as the most important. When we look at the last war between the two most powerful military nations in the world, we cannot fail to admit that the services which the German cavalry rendered by concealing the movements of the invading armies, by reconnoitring, and by harassing the enemy, were of far greater consequence than its performances on the battle-field.

Instead of relegating the cavalry to the rear of the marching columns, by a more rational employment of that arm the mass of the horsemen are thrown far in advance of an army, with the double object of concealing its numbers and movements, and of laying bare those of the enemy. To secure the first of these objects, the cavalry must form an impenetrable screen a good distance ahead of the main body of the army; to gain the second it must act with considerable boldness and enterprise, for a large measure of audacity is indispensable to explore to some purpose. In referring to the orders issued for the advance of the 5th and 6th Cavalry Divisions in July, 1870, the official account of the late Franco-German war expresses itself thus: "This body of cavalry was to establish itself at a short day's march on this side of the frontier, and from thence carry out constant enterprises against the enemy with squadrons and regiments, to keep an unflagging watch on the frontier, and to find and keep the touch of the enemy." *

The duties which the cavalry divisions have to perform may be summed up as follows:—

1. During the period of the strategical operations, to conceal the movements of the main body of the army on one hand, on the other to unveil those of the enemy.

2. In the battles, to act on the flanks and rear of the enemy, and to form a reserve at the disposal of the general commanding in chief.

3. At various times, to effect raids at a distance on the lines of communication and supply of the hostile army.

The cavalry has to watch and obtain information about the enemy, to ascertain the direction of his

* "German Official Account," vol. i. p. 73.

march, the strength and composition of his forces, and his intentions.

By a correct employment of this arm it therefore becomes possible for those who are responsible for the conduct of military operations to gauge the extent of the adversary's power and to fathom his designs.

The object of the cavalry covering the advance of an army is twofold—to conceal adroitly the situation and movements of the main columns, and, by keeping touch with the opponent's foremost troops, to procure for the commander-in-chief that constant information which he so urgently needs to direct in a becoming manner the operations of his army. Not only is the information gathered by troops specially trained for the purpose worthy of more credence than what we are likely to secure from other sources, but it is also of greater value, being that of the actual moment. This, however, is subject to two conditions—that the scouting parties are pushed forward as far as they can get, and that they transmit any item of relevant importance to the rear as swiftly as practicable, for from one moment to the other the circumstances are liable to undergo considerable alteration.

On the point of concealing the movements of the army, Von Schmidt expresses himself thus: "The more the enemy sees himself surrounded by 'points' and patrols only, which avoid him but constantly return again, and not by tangible bodies, the more certainly will every attempt he may make to break through be frustrated, and less will he be able to avoid perpetual observation and attain any information himself."

Colonel Borbstaedt makes the following observations on the action of the cavalry screen in 1870. "In advancing from the Sarre to the Moselle, the Second German Army was preceded by her cavalry divisions. On the 9th of August, the line forming a cordon, extended from Sarre-Union to Gross Tenquin, Faulquemont, Fouligny and Les Etangs, and their patrols pushed forward up to the neighbourhood of Metz. Thanks to this screen, which concealed their movements, the army corps, echelonned eight or ten leagues in rear, could perform their march in perfect security, without being subject to be brought to a sudden stand by the unexpected appearance of the enemy, or having to deploy unnecessarily. Moreover, the general-in-chief, by receiving numerous reports from all the cavalry patrols, could form an idea of the enemy's movements, and consequently direct his army corps in such a manner as to preclude useless marches and counter-marches."

The cavalry screen curtails the hardships of the outpost service, for an army which is well protected by its cavalry, will not only march, but will also repose with greater security. This security which the cavalry procures for the rest of the army is very valuable, inasmuch as it enables the bulk of the combatants to fight in the best of spirits and physical condition. A judicious employment of cavalry will prevent surprises, panics, wasteful marches, loss of time, useless efforts, and unnecessary fatigues. Indirectly the forward position assigned to this arm will secure other objects. It will give staff officers an opportunity for proceeding in advance of the columns to study the various positions, and to select suitable ground for camps or bivouacs; it will facilitate the alimentation of the main body, for the cavalry can serve requisitions for food, forage, and fuel for the troops that are coming up; and it will fill the population with a sense of the power, boldness, and confidence of their adversary, which will have great effect in preventing the inhabitants from taking up arms and rising to resist the invasion.

The bulk of the cavalry is now organized into independent divisions, generally composed of three brigades—two of light and one of heavy cavalry. The remaining squadrons are attached to the several infantry divisions of the army, to search their front, to foil any surprise, to prevent small detachments of the enemy's cavalry from approaching the advanced guards or overlooking the march of the columns, to keep up communication with the troops in front and in rear or with the lateral columns, and to furnish the necessary patrols and orderlies.

The term "independent cavalry divisions" was adopted to indicate that this portion of the cavalry has a special organization, is kept entirely separate from the heavy columns of the army, and acts under the immediate orders of the commander-in-chief. No army-corps commander has a right to interfere with the special task which he may assign to it, and so that all the information gathered by this source may reach him at as early a moment as practicable, it must go to him without filtering through other channels.

The cavalry divisions thus precede the main body of the army and cover its front and flanks. Whilst their object is to conceal from the adversary the dispositions and movement of their own army, they follow him step by step, harassing his forces, discovering his movements, and endeavouring to penetrate his intentions. The cavalry divisions must be early in the field, for they must act during the mobilization and concentration of the enemy. Being the first great units launched against the foe, they must be formed in peace and not improvised in war. Rightly handled, they will force him to abandon a vigorous offensive, from which he might have expected to reap signal advantages. As Baron v. d. Goltz very justly remarks, "the best tool for enabling one to take the initiative in a campaign is a numerous cavalry."

The battle of Vionville showed that cavalry is needed for other purposes than exploring and transmitting intelligence. A strong body of cavalry is a most valuable instrument, which a general may employ at a very pressing moment, either to hold a too venturesome enemy at a distance or to use offensively, so as to gain time for the arrival of other troops.

Daring enterprise adds to the force of an army; it inspires its ranks with self-confidence, while at the same time it generates despondency and want of assurance amongst the enemy's troops. Three-fourths of the power of cavalry lie in its moral effect, and the moral quantity of the two contending sides is never nicely balanced. One is confident, the other timid, and the confidence of the first increases with the timidity of the second; hence the saying that to expect defeat is nine-tenths of defeat itself. To be strong, the cavalry must be massed under the orders of its chief; to obtain success, it must act with rapidity and decision. As the side which acts with most vigour and rapidity will always secure the preponderance, a leader should press his enemy, sword in hand, from the very first, for thus only will his troops gain that moral superiority over their opponents which is so much desired. Nations which have a good and numerous cavalry, by constantly harassing the enemy, attain in the end its complete demoralization.

As a general rule, of two armies the one which can place the largest number of cavalry in the field has a great advantage over the other in all that relates to exploring and acquiring information. Exploring can only be done by troops which are able to move with great rapidity, which can go far in advance of the main body, and can retire speedily when threatened by superior forces. Cavalry is the only arm of the service which can do all this.

To conduct the exploration with good results is a difficult matter, and demands a thorough knowledge of all the objects which it is intended to attain. These are—

1. To discover the enemy, to gain touch of him, and to maintain the contact.

2. To cover thoroughly the main body of the army, to prevent the adversary from approaching it and thus getting an idea of its movements, or penetrating the intentions of its commander.

3. To pierce the adversary's screen, and obtain clear indications of his dispositions and designs.

4. To give timely notice to the troops in rear of any impending offensive movement.

5. To acquire a knowledge of a given district in all that relates to the characteristics of the ground, the condition of the communications, the nature and extent of the local resources, and the attitude of the population.

To gain useful information it is essential to be able to advance with a certain freedom in the enemy's direction; the exploring patrols, however, will meet with serious obstacles when a country is overrun by the unfriendly horsemen. This will render it necessary to search for the main body of the enemy's cavalry, to beat it and drive it back on its infantry. When this has been done, then it will be possible to conduct the scouting service with some prospect of success, as the enemy's screen will be pierced with little difficulty.

Now that the correct employment of cavalry has received a further illustration in the last Franco-German war, it is natural to foresee that in a future case the two contending forces will pursue the same tactics. It is this which has given rise to the general opinion that the next war will commence with a great and long cavalry contest. It cannot be otherwise, for it is impossible for two bodies of cavalry to keep close to each other without coming into contact; sooner or later the strongest of the two must drive the other away. This again indicates the necessity for being very strong in that arm.

Many officers have allowed themselves to be carried away by the enterprise displayed by the German cavalry in 1870, as if a new system had been discovered. In reality the German cavalry leaders only acted in conformity with the principles laid down by Frederick II., and pursued with such good results by the French cavalry in the Napoleonic wars. The adoption of the same method by both sides will not give the superiority so entirely to one, and will render, in future, clearing the way for an army more difficult than it was in 1870.*

* The action of the Russian cavalry in their last war was disappointing. Gourko employed his cavalry to some effect, but on the right flank reconnoitring was so badly performed that Osman Pasha's advance was not detected, and his sudden appearance at Plevna had all the elements of a surprise. In that war, on both sides, scouting was inefficiently performed.

The advantages in the matter of exploration will then rest with that side whose cavalry, being strongest and best handled, can succeed in driving the other off the field.

The events of the last Franco-German war have conveyed an exaggerated idea of the value of cavalry in getting relevant information. The German cavalry rendered important services in that direction, this no one will contest; but at that time it was apparently overlooked that what it was able to effect was mainly due to the negligence and utter want of enterprise on the part of the French. When in after years its action was calmly investigated and criticized by competent officers, it came to be recognized that in future it will possibly experience greater difficulties, as the enemy will naturally adopt the same system. The accuracy of the statement contained in the German Official Account, to the effect that the most weighty determinations of the commander-in-chief were always based on the clear and precise information which he received from his indefatigable cavalry, has been questioned. General Lewal * has endeavoured to prove that the German cavalry was seldom able to afford information on the most essential points. Many passages which occur in the German Official Account appear to show that, notwithstanding all the latitude accorded to the German cavalry, and the great enterprise shown by

* "Études de Guerre," par le General Lewal, vol. i. p. 95.

its officers, it often lost touch of the enemy and did not give the information which was most desired at a given moment. The army of the Crown Prince, as an instance, lost the touch of Marshal McMahon's army from the 6th to the 26th of August. In the second part of the campaign the German cavalry, after Bourges, could not furnish information of any particular consequence on the concentration of the French forces, because the Franctireurs prevented their penetrating to any distance.*

In the campaign of 1806 the French cavalry obtained greater successes than the German in 1870; it came up with the Prussian forces retiring in different directions, and compelled them to lay down their arms. These, the two most striking examples of the employment of cavalry in war in this century, have, however, been disappointing, as in neither case did the enemy's cavalry offer an adequate opposition.

The information the cavalry can obtain does not generally extend much beyond the surface of the enemy's army; the horsemen cannot penetrate beyond the opposing cavalry screen and see

* The "Revue de Cavalerie" for the month of April, 1895, contains an analysis of the exploration performed by the 5th German cavalry division on the 12th, 13th, and 14th of August, 1870, taken from the regimental records of six out of the nine regiments engaged. This analysis is worth studying, as it shows certain radical defects which were overshadowed at the time by the successful result of the general operations.

what movements are in actual course of preparation. The small detachments sent to observe can only exceptionally plunge into the centre of the enemy's forces, and find their way back with information of a most important nature.

As its principal occupation is to ascertain the whereabouts, movements, and dispositions of the hostile forces, the cavalry has not inappropriately been called the eyes of an army.

Some squadrons of each independent cavalry division are pushed forward to search for the enemy, scouring the country in every direction, feeling on every road, and ascending every eminence from which an extensive view can be obtained. The leading squads endeavour to discover the enemy's outposts, camps, or bivouacs, or its marching columns, which, once found, must be constantly kept in sight. To do this, the leading horsemen must conform with all the movements of the enemy, following him always when he retires, and falling back slowly on their supports when he presses them with superior numbers. Their object is not to fight, but to watch and report; consequently, though the cavalry patrols must ever be unrelaxing in their vigilance, their guiding rule is to abstain carefully from attacking or provoking a fight.

The most perplexing moment is when the adversary appears in considerable numbers. To eschew being cut off, they must conceal themselves, steal away quietly, and retire slowly on their supports; always being ready to resume their observation when the ground in front of them is clear.

A certain number of bold horsemen properly handled and ever hanging on the enemy will yield fruitful results. The ever-constant presence of these small parties of cavalry, and the knowledge of being incessantly watched, will disconcert the enemy; it will produce a torturing feeling of uneasiness, which in the long run cannot but generate a demoralizing effect. Some scouts in sight will evidently lead to the supposition that they are followed by powerful supports, which may of itself induce the adversary to fall back. If we only consider how difficult in war it is to get any reliable intelligence of the actual state of things, we can form an idea of how easily a bold party of horsemen can impose on the enemy. If nothing else, their statement that they are the advanced guard of a considerable force will meet with a large amount of credence; possibly no one will dare to inquire how far the main body is behind them.

Some French officers, who took part in the last Franco-German war, have depicted in a very forcible way the everlasting anxiety caused by the presence of the enemy's cavalry. General Vinoy,* referring to the action of the German cavalry, says, "From that moment we became the object of

* "Campagne 1870–71," "Siège de Paris," "Operations de 13e Corps."

continual and rapid inspection from the enemy's scouts. They kept galloping on our flanks, just out of range, seeking to see the head of our column and to calculate its force and report to their supports."

Colonel Bonie * gives a striking picture of the demoralizing effect which the appearance of the German horsemen produced after the retreat from the battle-field of Worth. "We received in the middle of the day of the 8th of August (at Sarrebourg) orders to saddle and mount, because the enemy's cavalry was in view. Some scouts were mistaken for the head of numerous columns; we then retired. From that moment until we reached Luneville their scouts watched us unceasingly. Linked to their army by horsemen, they gave an exact account of our position, of our halts, of our movements; and as they watched us from some little distance, incessantly appearing and disappearing, they spread uneasiness."

At Luneville, on the 10th of August, the French, when hoping to get a little rest, were suddenly ordered to march, for no other reason than because the enemy's cavalry was again in sight.

Further on, Colonel Bonie shows how quickly the Prussian staff found the lost track of Marshal McMahon's army. "But they quickly found us again by means of their cavalry, which never lost the touch, and marched on our flank, spread-

* "La Cavalerie Française, 1870."

ing out a curtain, behind which their army worked."

"At Chêne Populeux the enemy was thirty miles behind his cavalry. As we advanced we met groups of five or six horsemen, who retired slowly after examining our arrangements and informing those who followed them. If we wished to pursue, each fraction fell back on a support capable of resisting us and keeping us from penetrating the curtain. The service was so well performed by the Prussian cavalry,* that we marched, so to speak, within a net which enclosed us in its meshes."

The most remarkable thing in all this was that no cavalry officer on the French side became alive to the necessity for applying the lesson taught them by the Germans. For all that, we cannot believe that there were no officers in the French army who did not understand the correct employment of cavalry. In 1869—only a year before the war—one of their cavalry generals had published a fourth edition of De Brack's "Avant-Postes de Cavalerie Légère." † The writer of this very

* "The enemy concealed his movements so well behind the impenetrable screen of cavalry which he threw forward, that, in spite of the most persevering researches, it was never known where the main body of his force really was."—Napoleon III.

† In the discussion on a lecture delivered at the Royal United Service Institution, on the 18th of March, 1881, General Beauchamp Walker observed, "Captain Bell has adverted next to the 'Avant-Postes' of De Brack, which I always call my military bible, for it is about the most valuable book of study that has ever been written."

practical book was one of the most brilliant cavalry officers of the first empire. De Brack had been educated in the military school of Fontainebleau, and had gained great experience in war under such competent leaders as Lassale, Colbert, Montbrun, Maison, and Pajol. The very first page of his work contains in a few words the leading principles of the action of light cavalry.

"THE OBJECT OF LIGHT CAVALRY.

"*Q.* What is the object of light cavalry in a campaign?

"*A.* To shed light and protect the march of an army.

"*Q.* How can it attain that object?

"*A.* By preceding our columns, feeling on the flanks, surrounding and covering all with a vigilant and fearless curtain; following the enemy step by step, tormenting him, engendering uneasiness, discovering his projects, wearing out his forces in detail, and compelling him in short to waste in defence that offensive power from which he would otherwise have been able to derive the greatest advantages."

The best and most practical treatises are so much waste paper when the lessons they teach are not turned to account. When earnest men like De Brack, and many others whom we might name, write, they do not do so to advertise themselves, they are not actuated by a vain desire to expose their learning. They are impelled by a public spirit to place the personal experience they have acquired, and the result of their many days of meditation and study, at the disposal of their brother officers, for the good of the country, and for the honour of the army of which they have for many years formed part. Impressed as they fully are with the importance of the lessons of the past, their main desire is to see a thorough practical system established, and to eliminate, as far as it is possible, every chance of a repetition of former negligence, errors, and failures. All praise is due to such men. They have done more than their simple duty. It remains for those who have the direction of the military education of an army to do theirs, and to see that these salutary teachings are not allowed to remain fruitless, but are turned to profitable account.

It is strange how soon the teachings of war come to be forgotten. Frederick the Second and Napoleon understood the correct principles on which cavalry should be employed in the field; nevertheless, with time, both the Prussian and French cavalry leaders became oblivious of the principles laid down by these experienced commanders. Referring to the cavalry manœuvres held near Berlin in 1821—only six years after the conclusion of the war with France—von Kaeler points out how quickly the art of leading troops in the field is lost. How much more so must it be with the exploration, which cannot be fully rehearsed in mimic warfare.

It has been said that in the Jena campaign, outpost and reconnaissance duties were unknown to most of the Prussian officers. After 1866, they turned to account the fundamental lessons taught by Frederick and by Napoleon, which the French had quite forgotten; in 1870 they applied them with zeal and intelligence, and revived the *rôle* of cavalry in all that regards the exploration with singular success.

The cavalry should endeavour to penetrate as far as possible in the enemy's direction, without incurring serious risks. Small groups of three or four men each have a better chance of pushing unperceived across the enemy's outposts and between his columns than a larger body. They can more easily conceal their movements and get out of the enemy's way; they can be more daring, and, by skill combined with cunning, can make a rapid survey of the enemy's position and gather useful particulars. If threatened by superior numbers they can withdraw with facility, and, evading their pursuers, retire on their supports.

Boguslawski shows how the German cavalry carried out this practice in 1870. "If they found the way clear before them, they sent officers' patrols, with orders to push forward at any risk until they came upon the foe; . . . and if here and there a cavalry patrol, some days' march in advance of the division, was dispersed or cut off, one or two horsemen generally made their way back to give intelligence, which was what was wanted."

As a general rule, the exploring patrols should abstain from following the main thoroughfares, as these are more carefully watched. Their progress is less likely to be obstructed on the side roads and lanes. A small party of horsemen ably led can move by the most difficult paths; and just because cavalry are not expected to avail themselves of these byways, they have a better prospect of not meeting a soul to hinder their passage. Prudence enjoins their not remaining too long in the places they visit. A discreet leader will seek his information and disappear before the population have become aware of the smallness of his party and of the distance it is from its supports.

The well-known fact that an exploring patrol comprises a minimum of men, will suggest to the adversary the possibility of a surprise; consequently all due precaution must be observed to guard against ambushes. Where these may be expected, the troopers should follow each other at a distance of from 50 to 100 yards, the leader in the centre. Proceeding in this longitudinal formation, there is less risk of the whole party falling into ambush and being captured; at least one may effect his escape and convey information to the supports.

In exploring, the powers of the horses must be husbanded, for they will not only have to bear the weight of the rider for many consecutive hours, but they must be at any moment in a condition to launch out in a rapid gallop, when it is either required to keep up with the enemy or to slip away from him. Swiftness being one of the principal elements in exploring, we should not rest satisfied with selecting the best-mounted troopers, but should pay equal attention to their equipment. The soldier should march in the lightest possible order, for we cannot expect his horse to make long incursions at a very brisk pace, and bear heavy fatigues, if it is unnecessarily overloaded. The horse of a light cavalry man must not be looked upon as a beast of burden, but as a swift aid to locomotion, consequently it should be relieved of any articles which may retard its movements. For the time the troopers must be contented with what is absolutely indispensable. They must fare on what they can find—sometimes well, sometimes badly; being in very small numbers, their alimentation and that of their horses will seldom present any very serious difficulty.

All nations who make a considerable use of the horse carry a minimum of lumber. The most enterprising cavalries have lived on the local resources and have found sufficient means of subsistence.

The composition and strength of every exploring body must be proportionate to the task marked out for it. In war we have to discover what the adversary is in a position to do, and to find at the same time the best way for carrying our plans into execution. To this end, the front should be partitioned according to the number of large units, divisions and brigades available; a distinct zone being assigned to each, in which it should perform its operations.

Each cavalry division will thus be told off to explore a given tract of country. All alike will be preceded by detached squadrons, whose special mission will be, first, to advance until they have discovered the enemy; and, secondly, not to lose sight of him, shifting their ground as he moves from place to place, so as to be cognizant of his position at all moments. To obtain useful information it is not sufficient to catch an occasional glimpse of the enemy here and there; we must be constantly in touch with him. This action of never letting him get out of our sight, once he is found, is what we understand by the expression of keeping the contact.

To effect this, each foremost squadron must send a number of small patrols in the direction of the enemy. The most important of these patrols should be led by officers, who, owing to their superior attainments, can estimate without exaggeration the strength of the enemy's forces, and grasp the full purpose of their movements. This is nothing more than following our practice in the Peninsula war, only that two or three men are associated with each officer, so as to have one or two to keep a good look out, to be available for holding the horses when any of the party alight to make observations, or to convey information to the rear. These patrols, in point of fact, become so many small reconnaissances, for their leader is the real explorer of the party, the others are only joined to him to facilitate his task. The reconnaissances effected in this guise are the soul of the service of exploration.

As all these patrols have not the same relative consequence, the capacity of the individual who is to lead each one should be proportionate to the importance of its object. Officers, being too few in number to take charge of all the exploring patrols, will have frequently to be replaced by the most intelligent non-commissioned officers.

The number of patrols required to explore a given tract of territory thoroughly must always depend on the nature of the country, on the state of the atmosphere, on the strength and enterprise of the enemy. In any case, patrols must be sent in diverging directions at the same time; for, to obtain a multitude of reports, it is indispensable to gain touch of the enemy in many points.

No itinerary can be given to an exploring patrol, but simply the direction to be taken.

Impracticable as it will often be to follow a main road, which the adversary will keep more under observation, a skilful leader will be able to proceed in the direction assigned to him by following a tortuous course, alternating from side to side as the nature of the country and the folds of the ground offer more opportunities for concealment.

The exploring patrols have to seek for the enemy, to examine the country, and to hinder the circulation; performing thus the double service of informers and protectors. They summarily reconnoitre the country they travel over, and keep, as far as it lies in their power, the enemy's scouts and spies from crossing the screen. They must concern themselves, above all, about the enemy, and signal his presence, whether he be near or far away, in large or small numbers.

These widely disseminated groups, liable as they are to be overcome by a bold adversary, must be adequately supported by the contact squadrons they belong to. They must consequently look to their respective units for directions and assistance; they must be relieved, reinforced, or fall back on that unit, which is the contact squadron of which they form part. As exploring duties will cause considerable fatigue to both men and horses, the contact squadrons should be relieved by others from time to time.

The contact squadrons will follow their exploring patrols at a reasonable distance; behind them will come the reserve or main body of the division. To keep the enemy from tearing asunder the curtain which the cavalry thus forms with the object of concealing the movements of the army, a close connection must be maintained between these several bodies; the nearer the enemy is approached the closer the supports and the reserves must be brought to the foremost groups.

The very nature of the exploration will prevent these squadrons taking any notice of the movements of the main body of their division. The movements of the enemy must be their only guide; they must attach themselves to him, and stick to him tenaciously from the moment the touch comes to be established. The divisional commander must, nevertheless, be kept informed of the direction they are following, whenever, to keep touch with the enemy, they have to divert from the direction originally assigned to them.

The cavalry has, first, to gain the contact; secondly, to keep it. The maintenance of the contact consists in never losing sight of the adversary, in watching him whether he be stationary or on the march, in following all his movements, whether he be near or distant. As he must be subjected to an incessant scrutiny, the exploration must have all the elements of persistence, and should never be suspended or interrupted. There must be no intermission, and, if from any unforeseen occurrence the touch is lost, we must employ all our energies to regain it. This is a matter of such vital importance that every effort must be made to defeat any measures which a wily opponent may adopt to make us lose it. To surround the enemy with vigilant scouts, that will watch him without interruption, should be the first occupation of any officer sent to the front for the purpose of exploring; this he must do without waiting to receive orders.

Exploration is a laborious service, and it extends from the first day of a campaign to its very end. It must be continuous, without relaxation by day and by night, for if it were allowed to cease with daylight, during the many hours of darkness the enemy might disappear or draw near without our having the least conception of it. In 1870, before the battle of Vionville, we have a good illustration of the restless vigilance by which a body of cavalry should be animated. Mr. Archibald Forbes writes: "Probing about the front and flanks of the advance, the horsemen, under cover of night, had discovered where Bazaine's left flank lay in fancied security about the terrain villages, and the information went to the rear, we may depend, with all the speed that zealous men and stout horses could compass." * At night the exploring patrols should detach scouts to creep up on foot close to the enemy, to spy out, to listen,

* "My Experiences of the War between France and Germany," by A. Forbes.

and discover any alterations in his position or any preparations for movement.

A good arrangement for securing a continuity in the exploration is not to make the return of the patrols imperative. Frequent advancing and retiring only fatigues the men and horses; on this account, and not to have to do over again the same work on the following day, a certain amount of discretion should be allowed to the leaders of exploring patrols to remain in observation during the night in place of retracing their steps. This particularly recommends itself when the nature of the enemy's movements has unavoidably led a patrol to a considerable distance in advance of its squadron, and there is a fair prospect that by continuing where it is some important information may be gained.

In such an important service as exploration, the manner of acting must be clearly marked out, and not left entirely to individual option, for nothing is more disastrous in war than a want of method. As officers can effect a certain purpose by following different courses, it is not unreasonable to place a certain measure of confidence in their skill, for confidence well bestowed is seed sown on fruitful ground. Without quite stifling all initiative, it is nevertheless prudent to lay down all that is susceptible of being regulated. It will repay well to establish a system of procedure clear, simple, and based on past experience, which will prevent errors, omissions, and negligence.

A certain amount of freedom must necessarily be conceded to this arm, as without it all enterprise would be impossible ; this nevertheless must be done with judgment, not to suffer the cavalry to get out of hand.

To protect the flanks, and also to prevent small detachments getting round and molesting the troops on the march, the cavalry screen must occupy a larger front than the army itself. This must not be carried too far, or the screen will be so weakened that it will be easy for the enemy to break through. As by assuming a bold countenance a small body of troops can hold a greater one in check, a cavalry commander should strive to form a correct estimate of the strength of the enemy opposed to him, so as not to employ at any point a number of troops in excess of what is actually required. Real perfection in everything lies in obtaining important results by the employment of a just measure of means.

By failing to reconnoitre with his cavalry round the British flank on the forenoon of the day of Quatre Bras, Ney was led to believe that the allies were stronger than they were, and delayed his attack.

The great tenacity shown by Chanzy at Beaugency made Gambetta urge on Bourbaki the necessity for making a counter-attack on the army of Prince Frederick Charles. On the 9th of December an order was sent to the general to march on Blois, but he not only refused to do so, but demanded instead to be permitted to retire his troops as far as Saint-Amand-Montrond. At that period there were only south of Orleans, as far as Gien and Vierzon, some small detachments of Prince Frederick Charles's army, consisting principally of cavalry, for the prince had marched the bulk of his forces to the west, where a decisive action against Chanzy had become urgent. The bold countenance showed by these weak detachments of cavalry imposed on General Bourbaki, and kept three army corps inactive at a pressing moment.

A point to be studiously guarded against is a too large dissemination of the cavalry, which might render its concentration very difficult or tardy if attacked by the enemy's cavalry, or if required suddenly for any offensive movement. In the war of 1870–71 the German cavalry displayed great enterprise; the French did not. When both sides will, however, resort to the same tactics—as will surely be the case in the next great war—there will be more need for having to concentrate rapidly to check an irruption of the enemy's horsemen. This will lead to the cavalry divisions being kept more together, and scouting on a smaller front.*

To maintain touch with the enemy must

* In 1870–71 a German cavalry division spread out as far as 21 miles. The best authorities are now of opinion that from $9\frac{1}{3}$ to $12\frac{1}{2}$ miles should be the maximum front for exploration per division, and that the distance between the independent divisions and the head of the following columns should not be more than from $15\frac{2}{3}$ to 19 miles.

naturally lead to the dispersion of a given body, for the exploration, as we have said, must cover a certain extent of ground when our object is to gather information on many points. This dispersion assumes that the enemy is equally disseminated; however, we have never a certitude on which to base such a supposition, and, if the adversary has massed his forces and moves rapidly to attack, a scattered division may not have sufficient time for concentrating. The enemy's cavalry can only be overcome by a rapid concentration. When within striking distance of the foe, the commander of a cavalry division must, consequently, be prepared to concentrate the whole of his forces as quickly as possible, following the leading principle of war, which enjoins to operate with all our forces united.

The object of the cavalry divisions is to see what the enemy is doing, and to prevent his seeing what we are about. For the first the cavalry must necessarily extend on a wide front; for the second it must concentrate and fight. The exploration, therefore, should not be overdone to the detriment of a rapid concentration.

As the more a body of cavalry is numerous and united the greater is the prospect of its gaining an advantage on the enemy, it will be prudent not to employ too many detachments. Each division should keep as much as possible together, sending ahead one or more squadrons to undertake the exploration, and echelonning in the rear only what is strictly necessary to pass the information as it comes to hand.

A division would thus follow the principal thoroughfare leading towards the enemy in the region assigned to it for exploration, all the lateral roads being reconnoitred by patrols commanded by an officer or a non-commissioned officer. What is of great moment is for all portions of a cavalry division, whether at rest or on the march, to be well connected together, and for the information of every particular which has been observed or heard regarding the enemy to be speedily brought to the notice of any detached parties. Intelligent scouts will give timely notice of the enemy's movements, and on their information it will be generally possible to gauge his intentions with approaching accuracy. Should he succeed in breaking through the curtain, the direction of his march will be known betimes, and dispositions can be taken to attack him in flank or in rear, and cut off his retreat.

Some writers have given a normal formation for the march of a cavalry division. As the nature of the country, the number and direction of the roads, and the attitude of the enemy, must always be taken into account, no hard and fast rules can be laid down. The movements of a cavalry division must be as elastic as possible, and the talent of its leader lies in making the formation accord with the existing circumstances.

Capturing some prisoners is a matter of considerable consequence, on account of the prospect there is of being able to draw more or less relevant news from their statements. The uniforms of the prisoners and of the dead will reveal in an indirect manner the strength of the enemy. From the best information it can collect, the intelligence staff will be in a position to draw up an order of battle of the adversary's army; the uniforms of certain regiments will afterwards indicate in a very positive manner what corps are occupying a certain region of the country, and when it is known that these form part of certain brigades, divisions, and army corps, the inference can be drawn that those units are somewhere in the neighbourhood. As this comes to be ascertained all along the enemy's front, there will be little difficulty in fixing with tolerable accuracy the location of the various army corps.

The following illustration of an instance which occurred in 1815 is given by Comte D'Herisson in "Le Cabinet Noir." "Quite early on the day of the battle of Waterloo an officer was despatched by General Grouchy, son of the marshal, to requisition food in the neighbouring villages. This officer returned and informed him that he had fallen in with some Prussians, who had hindered him. Mons. de Grouchy concluded that they must have belonged to Blücher's troops marching to join Wellington, and the matter appeared to him so important that he set spurs to his horse to get at the emperor. At about ten o'clock he was with Soult, to whom he communicated the circumstances.

"Soult advised him to go in person and inform the emperor. The latter having heard him, said, 'Who is the stupid officer who could make a similar report? The Prussians are very far from here.' Mons. de Grouchy returned to his brigade, and after repeating to the officer the emperor's remarks, told him that it was necessary to lay hold of some prisoners. The officer set out with a few volunteers, and Mons. de Grouchy marched to support him. Soon two foot soldiers and a hussar were captured, and Mons. de Grouchy hastened to convey them to the chief of the staff.

"The emperor had them interrogated, and it was consequent on their statement that they formed part of Guttien's and Schmidt's brigades, that he was led to order Mouton to march so as to cover his right. It was then nearly two o'clock."

A good deal has been said of the boldness of the German horsemen in the last Franco-German war, nevertheless the following passage taken from Baron Marbot's memoirs* shows what services our officers rendered to the Duke of Wellington in the Peninsula war. "During our stay at Sobral, I saw another artifice employed by the English, and one of sufficient importance to be worth noting.

* Baron Marbot's "Memoirs," chap. xv. p. 130.

It is often said that thoroughbred horses are of no use in war, because their price is so high and they require so much care that it would be almost impossible to provide a squadron, much more a regiment, with them. Nor indeed do the English use them on campaign ; but they have a habit of sending single officers, mounted on fast thoroughbreds, to watch the movements of a hostile army. These officers get within the enemy's cantonments, cross his line of march, keep for days on the flanks of his columns, always just out of range, till they can form a clear idea of his numbers, and the direction of his march. After our entry into Portugal we frequently saw observers of this kind flitting round us. It was vain to give chase to them, even with the best mounted horsemen. The moment the English officer saw any such approach, he would set spurs to his steed, and nimbly clearing ditches, hedges, even brooks, he would make off at such speed that our men soon lost sight of him, and perhaps saw him soon after a league further on, note-book in hand, at the top of some hillock, continuing his observations. This practice, which I never saw any one employ like the English, and which I tried to imitate during the Russian campaign, might perhaps have saved Napoleon at Waterloo by affording him a warning of the arrival of the Prussians. Anyhow, these English 'runners,' who were the despair of the French general from the moment we left Spain, increased in boldness and cunning as soon as we were in front of Sobral. One could see them come out of the lines and race with the speed of stags through the vines and over the rocks to inspect the position occupied by our troops." *

In all this the habit of riding across country and taking part in races and steeple-chases—which should always be encouraged—gives our officers a considerable advantage. Naturally the greater range and accuracy of modern fire-arms will render such practice in future more dangerous; for all that, the great improvement made in the power and portability of field-glasses will still enable an officer to make his observations, though precluded from approaching as close to the enemy as heretofore.

After reading of the enterprise of our officers in the Peninsula war, as commended by one of their adversaries, one may recall with just indignation how, in the last contest which occurred in England, Feversham, with 700 cavalry at his command, failed to ascertain what the rebels were about at Bridgewater, only three miles from his camp. There was no excuse whatsoever for his utter want of energy in a struggle with raw levies, led by a

* In the Peninsula, British officers could do this unsupported, as they were campaigning in a friendly country. To explore thus, or with small patrols, will bear no fruit if the enemy has a large quantity of light cavalry, and the population is bold. In the second part of the last Franco-German war, the German exploring parties could not display the same audacity as they had exhibited in the earlier days of the campaign.

wavering chief, in which it is related that there were traitors in both camps ready to supply the opposite side with information.

It is a fact which has often been adduced, that in 1859 and in 1866, owing to inadequate reconnoitring, the French and the Prussian staffs entertained no suspicion of the near and concentrated presence of the Austrian forces.

The leader of a cavalry detachment should never allow anything to escape his notice; his inquisitiveness should never cease. When the preparations for an attack on Orleans, in November, 1870, were in a very forward stage, Mons. Thiers returned to Tours from the Prussian headquarters. It was feared that the Prussian escort, seeing the position and the activity of the French outposts, would warn their chiefs that some important movement was in contemplation. Fortunately for the French, the escort returned to Orleans without entertaining any suspicion of what was intended.

In all that relates to exploration, we must never lose sight of the fact that our adversary will employ the same means as we do. The information which we shall strive to gain on all that relates to his strength, his movements, his condition is just what he will seek in return by using analogous measures. Our task is therefore double, to gain intelligence of his power and intentions, and to prevent him from knowing ours.

Whether the army is halting or moving, the

cavalry screen has the same duties to perform; in both cases it must display the same vigilance in covering the main body, in watching the action of the enemy in its front, and collecting information. Its heaviest work will occur in the opening part of the campaign, for, naturally, as the two contending armies close on each other, even the cavalry which has remained victorious in the cavalry combat, will not be sufficient to act by itself, and will have to pause and wait for the co-operation of the other arms. At that period it can be directed on the enemy's flanks and rear, to threaten his communications, to capture his convoys, to destroy his magazines, and to damage his railway lines of supply. These later operations, however, come more properly under the heading of cavalry raids.

A bold cavalry dash, designed to effect some special object, may conduce to important results. On the 20th of July, 1870, as an example, a detachment of 30 Rhineland Uhlans, under Lieutenant Voight, destroyed a viaduct of considerable height on the railway line which connects Metz with Saarguemines, Bitche, Hagenau, and Strasburg. These irruptions, nevertheless, cannot always be carried out with impunity. On the 12th of August of the same year a feeble party of the 10th Dragoons, consisting of one officer, Lieutenant v. Toll, two non-commissioned officers, and 29 rank and file, were sent to Pont-à-Mousson with the object of damaging the railway and telegraph. At

Pont-à-Mousson this party fell in with Captain de Thauvenay of the staff of the Xth Corps, who, escorted by two platoons of the 17th Hussars, was effecting a reconnaissance.

Having taken what appeared to him sufficient measures of security, by posting squads and vedettes to give the alarm in case the enemy should appear, Lieutenant v. Toll ordered his men to dismount and set to work. The hussars remained in the town.

The telegraph-posts were demolished, and with much labour one of the rails had been removed, when the alarm was raised, for bodies of French cavalry were seen tearing down the line at a swift gallop. The enemy—belonging to the 1st and 3rd Regiments of Chasseurs d'Afrique—also emerged from the town and attacked the dragoons in rear before they had time to mount. With difficulty Lieutenant v. Toll, the trumpeter, and thirteen dragoons managed to effect their retreat and rejoined the regiment at Silly-en-Saulnois; the rest were either killed, drowned, or captured. Of the party under Captain de Thauvenay, he escaped, but almost all the hussars, officers, non-commissioned officers, and men, were captured.

As the artillery comes into action, the cavalry, having performed its preliminary *rôle*, must clear the front. It will then be located on the flanks to aid the other arms in the battle, to seize what opportunities may offer themselves, to gain timely information of the advance of any of the enemy's army corps to participate in the contest, to turn a defeat into a rout,* and to take up the touch, so as to ascertain the real direction of the enemy's retreat. The last point is of the greatest consequence, for experience shows that time lost is never regained. After the battle of Austerlitz, the French army pursued the Austro-Russian forces on the wrong road; because Murat's cavalry had mistaken the enemy's line of retreat. At break of day on the 3rd of December, Murat was sent with 72 squadrons in pursuit, but he followed the Olmutz road, and neglected to scour the others. Had the French cavalry after the battle of Ligny kept touch with the defeated Prussians, Napoleon would not have been kept in ignorance of the real direction their columns had taken. It was almost night on the 16th of June when the Prussians began to retire from the battle-field, but Grouchy only started in pursuit on the following afternoon.

The attention of the cavalry must not be allowed to be distracted by passing events, and the battle going on is no reason for suspending the exploration. Had Du Barrail's reserve cavalry explored during the battle of Gravelotte, it would have given timely notice of the approach of a German corps by the Conflans-Moineville road, and revealed that the

* Jomini observes, "An army deficient in cavalry rarely obtains a great victory." This is easily explained, for such an army lacks the means for turning a defeat into a rout, through a vigorous and unrelenting pursuit. A victory secures comparatively very small results unless it can be turned into a crushing defeat.

real object of the Germans was to throw back the French right into Metz. The scrutiny of the enemy must not cease for a moment, for if it is once interrupted it is difficult to resume. In the last incidents of the fight, above all, it must be carried out with the greatest activity, so as to establish the right direction of the adversary's retreat.

To regain the contact and to ascertain the true line of retreat after a battle is a difficult matter, for the adversary employs his rear-guard to stay the progress of the victors and to conceal the direction followed by his forces, which he often changes after having got some way from the battle-field. At Austerlitz, at the Moskowa, at Ligny, at Koeniggraetz, at Reichshoffen, at Spicheren, at Borny, and at Orleans, in each case the cavalry lost the contact, as the exploration had been suspended during the battle. After the battle of Koeniggraetz the contact was not entirely re-established until the sixth day. The exhaustion of the troops after a long and hard-contested engagement apparently causes a certain delay before an organized pursuit can commence.

The cavalry will be posted on the wings, which it must protect during the battle. This arm must give timely notice of any turning movements, it must obtain useful information, for what is above all necessary at this time is to know what occurs in the enemy's rear. All this a cavalry leader must do on his own initiative, without waiting for orders. A certain number of intelligent scouts should be directed to occupy every point of vantage which overlooks the enemy's position, to prowl about his flanks, approaching as close as they can and examining all his actions.

As the enemy's resistance shows signs of giving way, orders must be given for the cavalry to get ready to follow in pursuit. Any hesitation or delay at this moment may entail the loss of the best fruits of a victory.

To bear good results the pursuit must be guided by an intelligent exploration. The flanks of a retreat are very favourable for observation, and exploring patrols should be pushed in these directions. The least fatigued of the cavalry should follow the defeated forces and ascertain the direction which they have taken, sending frequent reports to the rear of all traces of the enemy. The main body can follow on the information thus acquired. A direct pursuit will never offer such good results as one executed on the flanks. In the former there is always a prospect of its being checked by the enemy's rear-guard, whereas by pursuing on the flanks the cavalry may outreach the enemy at certain defiles and retard his retreat. Troops retiring from a lost battle-field march fast, and can only be outstripped by cavalry sent to a considerable distance.

Murat, in 1806, after the battles of Jena and Auerstadt, gave a fine illustration of a cavalry pursuit. The movements of his squadrons were vigorous and daring even to temerity.

In covering a retreat, small detached parties of cavalry should ascertain the pursuer's strength and intentions. This reconnoitring during a retreat is often neglected, and enables the pursuing cavalry to reap signal advantages from its enterprise.

Much has been written during the past few years on the future *rôle* of cavalry, on the marching formation best adapted for a cavalry division, on the extent of front which it can efficiently explore, on the most rational way for supporting the most forward exploring patrols, on the necessity for combining the exploration with a rapid concentration to make head against the enemy. On many of these points the writers are not of accord, their opinions are conflicting, and a good deal appears not to have been conclusively determined. It is beyond our powers to go deeply into these matters, which have been treated already at great length by competent and talented officers. The limit of this work allows us to do no more than to indicate the elementary principles of cavalry exploration; for a more searching inquiry into the subject, the military student should consult such works as treat on the strategic service of cavalry and on cavalry tactics as a speciality.

CHAPTER V.

TRAINING OF CAVALRY IN EXPLORING DUTIES.

CAVALRY wanting in rapidity, boldness, and dash is not of much good in war. The motto, *celer et audax*, does not, however, comprise all that it should be, for quickness and boldness are not sufficient, and the worth of this arm will always be proportionate to the pains which have been taken in everything which forms part of its training. The most daring bravery, the greatest enterprise displayed by the leader of a cavalry detachment, in place of being useful, may be hurtful, when from a want of knowledge on his part he is not able to form a right appreciation of the actual circumstances, or can assign the exact interpretation to what comes under his observation.

The training of cavalry outside the parade ground should be eminently practical. In time of peace it is too much confined to smartness in appearance, precision in field movements and other drills; that arm is not sufficiently habituated to such exercises as are analogous to what it would have to perform in a campaign. Men must be trained in peace for what they will have to do in war; but how is it possible that the latter exercises can become a thoroughly practical training, if they are made secondary in importance to the former and are not constantly repeated.

Reconnoitring and exploring work cannot be practised within the narrow limits of a drill field; for this we need a large extent of country, of a varied nature, and intersected by plenty of roads; for we must bear in mind that in war a single regiment will have to spread out and explore on a front extending for several miles. We will not say that the utter dissimilarity between peace and war, that the scattered state of our garrisons, that the want of suitable ground in our enclosed country—coupled with the unwillingness of our farmers to lend us the use of their fields—do not militate against the frequent performance of this valuable training; nevertheless, we think that this may also often be traced to a forgetfulness of the most essential work which the cavalry will be called upon to execute in war.

An army is not kept up for show, but for use; consequently every hour taken from instructing the troops in such duties as they will have to perform in the field is a loss of valuable time to the country. That excessive grooming of our horses, which renders them too delicate to bear exposure and hardships on service, that unceasing furbishing and cleaning, which disgusts the soldier, might with good reason be replaced by more profitable training. One should always judge by results, and we have seen cavalry, which in appearance could not compare with ours, acquit itself in the field in a manner which has elicited the admiration of our smartest cavalry commanders.

In his estimate of the light cavalries of Europe, De Brack makes the following observations on our cavalry: "If the British cavalry understood war, it might possibly be, in the day of battle, the most terrible in Europe; its well-established luxury in horses, in equipment, harmonizes with the courage and fine presence of its soldiers; when it comes in sight you may be sure that its movements are well combined, that its attack will be powerful and its retreat regular. It seldom parts company with its infantry, which insures its rest in the bivouacs. It looks after the position and gauges the dispositions of the enemy more by means of well-paid spies than through its own reconnaissances."

Cavalry requires a very able body of officers, and not empty-headed dandies; it must have men who combine with physical courage, which masters dangers, a full sense of their responsibilities. Its officers need to be more highly educated than those of the other arms, not only because they have more opportunities of acting independently, but because their incidents are more fleeting, and one of the principal duties they will have to perform may have a great consequence on the result of a campaign. A cavalry officer should reflect that it is not sufficient for him to look after the condition of his men and of his horses, and to be prompt, vigilant, and fearless, for the exact measure of his efficiency on service will always be proportionate to the knowledge he has acquired of the higher branches of his profession. This knowledge should comprise a very thorough acquaintance with the duty of covering an army in the field, which is without question the most important work which the cavalry will have to undertake in a campaign.

De Brack very justly observes: "No condition demands so many natural dispositions, an inborn genius for war, so much as that of an officer of light troops.* The qualities which make the superior man—intelligence, will, and force—must be found united in him. Constantly having to depend on himself, exposed to frequent encounters, answerable not only for the band which he leads, but also for the troops which he protects and enlightens, the

* Through pure extravagance our cavalry is closed to many officers who are by nature eminently adapted for that arm. Out of a number of young gentlemen who pass yearly into the army, the cavalry take many who have no better qualification than the large amount of their private income. Not seldom, to get the required number, commissions are bestowed on youths who have not scored sufficient marks in a competitive (?) examination. Any one who will take the trouble to analyze the expenses of our cavalry officers can only come to one conclusion, which is that the largest portion of their income goes to meet what we may call non-compulsory expenses.

employment of his moral and physical faculties are always in demand."

The art of war, with its principles and problems, with all its numerous and intricate details, must be learnt just the same as any other profession. We might say even with greater diligence, as the occasions for putting the lessons to a practical test are, fortunately, rare. It is impossible, therefore, to combat too strongly the idea that a minimum of work and a maximum of expensive amusement constitute the proper thing in an officer's life. In every career alike it needs industry and time to acquire glory, or even to make one's self a name.

It requires a very high sense of duty to make young officers, full of life and with ample means for satisfying their natural inclinations for enjoyment and pastime, chain themselves to their desk to ponder for hours on works treating on war. Far be it from us to wish to see too many bookworms in our ranks, for there never was a truer maxim than "all work and no play makes Jack a dull boy." For war we do not want dull boys or mere theorists, we need men full of health, strength, and energy. What we, nevertheless, desire to impress on all officers is, that personal strength and courage alone are not sufficient to secure distinction in the field; and that bravery, to be of any avail, must be combined with a fair knowledge of war. In a well-regulated life there is time for everything, and an officer, who is so inclined, will always find in the twenty-four hours time for study and leisure for recreation.

A cavalry officer would do well to prepare himself, above all, for those duties which call for the exercise of the eye, ear, and mind; to accustom himself to reflect on what must be of the greatest moment for the commander-in-chief to know, and to learn how to interpret correctly the several indications which the enemy may afford. Let us bear in mind that a single item of relevant information, given in the nick of time, may have such important consequence on the result of certain operations, as to make the reputation of the officer who supplies it. It may otherwise be the means of procuring him further opportunities.

Some knowledge of this nature may be acquired by practising the war game, some may be picked up in peace manœuvres, other can only be gathered by reading diligently and impressing on the mind the details of past campaigns.

The command of a reconnoitring patrol is the most important duty which will fall to a cavalry subaltern in war, and will offer him opportunities for bringing himself to the notice of his superiors. This duty can, however, only be performed efficiently by an officer who has qualified himself for it in time of peace.* To be a bold rider across country,

* Some few years ago General de Gallifet, referring to his own army, stated that there were very few officers who united in themselves all the necessary conditions for a good leader of an exploring patrol.

though a very necessary qualification, is not all; to this must be added skill and artifice, so as to delude observation and to know whether to brave the enemy or to retire before him, and, in the latter case, how to act so as to lead the adversary into error. It will need more than ordinary courage for an officer, backed by a handful of troopers, to plunge in the midst of a country overrun by the enemy and face the unknown. Many of us know how the dread pause in waiting for hostilities to commence, when confronting a hostile army, tries the courage of most men; for, however prepared we may be to brave a danger which we can see, we are disturbed by a danger which threatens us, but which we cannot clearly discern.

War is such a thorough oversetting of the normal state of things, that whatever we may do, it is impossible to devise any system in peace which will be even a faint reproduction of a state of war. The absence of the most embarrassing conditions which are found in the field, makes the rehearsal of the work to be performed in war fall ever so far short of the real thing, that the instruction imparted in the drill season and in the yearly manœuvres cannot but naturally be very incomplete. The dearly purchased experience of service in the field alone, is rightly admitted to be the best teacher of war; this experience, however—not only with regard to the cavalry, but also to the other arms—

is not always at our command, and in our days campaigns are too rapid to allow sufficient time for gaining it. Study is not a thorough substitute for it, but it will go far towards instilling in the minds of the officers those maxims which will have to guide their actions in war.

Our usual wars * afford very little real instruction for our cavalry. The enemy's training is of a rude and primitive order, he is not led by highly educated, enterprising, and ambitious officers; and, whilst the number of horsemen we employ is small in proportion to the other arms, the adversary often takes the field without any. From all these causes it follows that our cavalry officers must gather their lessons from an intelligent study of the history of the great wars which have occurred in the past.

Before taking the field they should have received a far-reaching theoretical and practical training. Without it it will be impossible to expect them to feel properly for the enemy, to explore in accordance with the ideas of the general commanding, and to

* Our ordinary contests are an unsatisfactory experience, for they are carried out against enemies who, brave as they may be, lack a sound military organization, efficient arms, and dexterous leaders. The science being all on one side, they are not a fair trial of skill between two accomplished captains. Were we simply to place our trust on the ease with which we overcome our usual opponents, we would be laying ourselves open to some very cruel experiences, were we at any time to meet a foe which in point of organization, training, and leading is equal if not better than ourselves.

render a clear and true account of what comes under their observation.

A cavalry officer must see all he can and get to know all there is to be known; his perception must be clear and his judgment sound. It is not sufficient for an officer to see, but he must see well,* he must have what is called a military *coup d'œil* to estimate circumstances at their just value. Without it he might furnish his chief with erroneous intelligence. The accuracy of the information he gives is a most important point, for it is on this that the commander-in-chief arranges his plans and moves.

When both contending armies have good enterprising cavalry officers, who are thoroughly masters of the *rôle* which is assigned to their arm, it will be by no means an easy matter to secure relevant information. To draw correct conclusions it is essential to ascertain where the bulk of the opposing forces are, what is their number, and what they are in a condition to do. This is just what the adversary will endeavour to keep from our knowledge through his cavalry screen, through his outposts, and through other precautionary measures.

* Not only should a light and powerful binocular, which will give to the organs of vision a greater range and a more distinct field, form part of every officer's equipment, but it should be supplied in a given proportion to all parties sent out to observe the enemy. Aitchison's patent pocket binocular, which closes into a small space and is very light, only weighing 5 oz., appears very well adapted for service in the field.

The necessity already noticed for having officers who are acquainted with the language spoken in the theatre of operations applies more to the cavalry than to the other arms. Without a knowledge of the vernacular, it is obvious that much of the information which it is possible to gather from the inhabitants, prisoners, or deserters, will be lost.

Cavalry officers and non-commissioned officers should also be very expert in reading a map. The advantages which this knowledge will confer when moving through a strange country cannot be overrated. Without good maps it will be nigh impossible to cover an army with anything like efficiency.

When troops take the field every endeavour will be made to furnish them with the best maps procurable. Of late years the importance assigned to military topography has been somewhat overdone. What is of greater moment than to produce an intelligent sketch is, that the officers and non-commissioned officers shall be expert in reading a map, shall be able to find their way about a country by its aid, and shall know how to correct it and bring old information up to date.

To keep touch with the enemy and to apprise the general commanding of his doings, is only a part of the officers' work; in the execution of this duty they will become acquainted with the characteristics and state of the country they have explored, which should always be incorporated in their reports. However accurate the maps in possession may be, a country may at any time be affected by some special circumstances. The information which they give is the normal, but any disturbance of the normal may render certain military operations difficult or even impracticable. Heavy rains may swell torrents and render fordable rivers impassable, may flood a large tract of land or make the roads heavy and unfit for guns and transport wagons. Bridges may have been destroyed, villages may have been burnt, etc. It is always of the greatest importance for a commander to know the actual conditions of the country at the moment, and these can only be ascertained by personal observation. The cavalry being pushed far in advance of the main body, becomes the best medium for procuring precise information of this nature.

All officers who are sent out to reconnoitre should note on their reports the nature of the roads and of the country, stating if the roads are practicable for artillery and transport. The condition of the soil, if dry or wet, hard or soft, may have a certain influence on the march of the columns, for, when the ground is favourable, troops may move across country over the fields independent of roads. The actual state of the latter, moreover, requires to be known, so as to regulate the length of the marches in such a manner as to spare the troops all unnecessary fatigue. Maps are often destitute of certain particulars which may be useful to a commander; many by-paths and tracks are left out, the nature of the fords is not indicated, all recent constructions, new plantations, and improvements have not yet been inserted, and information on these minor details may often be of the greatest value.

Amongst the principal requisites for a cavalry officer we may enumerate a good eyesight, a clear appreciation of ground, familiarity with the enemy's language, and an intimate knowledge of the marching formations and general composition of the different fighting units of an army. Courage, skill, and presence of mind are the three great qualities which form the man of action. To baffle all manner of dangers, to make up in audacity for the want of numbers, the officer must have experience of war, natural genius, and mental powers to arrive at rapid decisions and execute them with skill and vigour. In the absence of actual war experience, we must strive to develop his resolution, activity, and sagacity by a sound practical training. Officers who are exercised in exploring duties in the yearly manœuvres will be found to take a keen interest in this work.

Just as it is indispensable for the officer to possess a very high standard of knowledge, so does the training of the trooper call for considerable care. An efficient exploration can only be undertaken by troops who have been made to understand its principles, and who have been frequently exercised with that object. It would be certainly unreasonable to expect the soldier to learn this work in the field, for in a very few days he will come into contact with the enemy. In ordinary field movements the trooper performs mechanical work, and has to comply with the commands of his troop or squadron leaders; in the field he has often to rely on his individual intelligence, and has no one to guide him. The development of his mind can only be the result of constant practice, and we certainly cannot look for it when the soldier has for years been broken to simple passive obedience.

The troop officers must themselves train their men, for it is of great consequence for them to know the individual character of each soldier. They must endeavour to make themselves competent teachers, a thing which does not come easy to every one alike. All through his training the trooper must be impressed with the advantages which his sagacity and vigilance will confer on his army. The very fact that the non-commissioned officers will often have to replace the officers is a strong reason for taking extra pains in training them in everything which regards the acquisition of information, so as to form them into efficient leaders of exploring patrols.

The men should be frequently exercised in exploring. In their marches, in field days, in the annual manœuvres, their officers should take every opportunity to make the soldiers familiar with the country. They should be instructed how to find their way by the assistance of a map, their direction by the height of the sun by day, and by the polar star by night. They should be sent in different quarters to ascertain the names of the various villages and localities, to learn the direction and condition of the different roads, to gather particulars about rivers and other water-courses, on the situation of bridges, on the nature of the fords, on the extent of woods, morasses and enclosed properties, on the location of defiles. They should be taught how to render a faithful account of all that they have been directed to ascertain, and in what shape they should present the information they have gathered. This instruction should comprise both day and night work.

It is not simply sufficient for the men to know the kind of information that they will have to go in quest of, they must be made fully alive to the fact that to observe well it is indispensable to eschew every possibility of being detected. They must consequently be impressed with the necessity for concealing their movements, for taking every advantage of existing cover, for ascending every eminence from which it is possible to obtain an extended view of the country in front. They should know how in doing the latter they should alight before reaching the brow of a hill, for a mounted man forms a conspicuous object on the sky-line, and can be seen from a great distance. They must be taught to pay attention to all indications, footprints, fires, smoke, dust, the glitter of arms, the rumbling noise of vehicles, the sounds of instruments, etc., and how any of these symptoms must be at once communicated to their leader.

It does not appear to us that sufficient attention has been paid to the necessity for teaching cavalry to dismount and conduct their exploration on foot. An obstacle which his horse cannot possibly overcome should never put a period to the fulfilment of an explorer's duty; the trooper should know that in such a case he should dismount, advance on foot, seek some favourable point of view, make his observations, then regain his horse and rejoin his party. The more, in short, the ordinary conditions of the soldier differ from the circumstances of war, the more it becomes necessary to educate him diligently on these and similar points.

To render the instruction more thorough, and to teach the soldier how to overcome the difficulties which he will have to contend against on active service, one squadron or one regiment can be made to work against another. It will enhance the value of this practice if each lesson is repeated, after the errors committed have been explained to the troops. If the reconnoitring and scouting practice can be carried out for several days in succession, there will be a greater resemblance to the actual conditions of war.

Before being exercised in the open, the soldier should know the why and wherefore of everything he will have to do, for there is seldom sufficient time for entering into lengthy explanations on the exercising ground. Theoretical instruction and catechising should always form the prelude of all out-of-door training, and this can be substituted for field drills when the weather is inclement.

As all ranks will have in their turn to take part in the exploration,* great pains should be taken in teaching them what they will have principally to look for, and the manner in which they should communicate what comes to their notice. The habit of practising cavalry in this duty in peace will bear fruit in war, for, without a considerable training of this kind, both officers and men will to a certainty experience many difficulties at the most critical period of a campaign, viz. at its commencement.

When this is properly attended to, the men will be made familiar with all those indications which portend the immediate vicinity of the enemy, with the proper manner of acting once they have sighted him, and with the right kind of information

* Some writers are in favour of having in each squadron some men especially trained for scouting work; we think that all troopers should be trained in it alike. It will then rest with the officers to select at any time the most intelligent men to employ on this duty.

which it is necessary to pass instantly to the rear. It will then be unnecessary to point out every day to each individual the objects on which he should concentrate his attention. His training should have taught him all that he will be expected to report on general grounds; with regard to any special points on which the general commanding may desire to be made acquainted, instructions can only be given at the time. The officers will have to direct the men's attention to these particulars, and, if they are of weighty consequence, it will induce them to detail the most intelligent and sharp men out of their troop.

In watching the enemy in any one point it is not advisable to employ too many men; two or three intelligent and well-mounted troopers will be sufficient to see and pass all relevant particulars to the nearest detachment. A larger party would draw attention without acquiring any more information. The men and horses must be spared all unnecessary fatigue; consequently, when a small post can keep an eye over a large tract of country, it would be pure waste to employ several parties.

As a general rule there is always a great inclination to employ too many men. Cavalry cannot be wasted, and the right principle is to use not more of it than is actually required to gain the end in view. Instead of sending a large body, it is more profitable to send a few small ones; for, as these follow different directions, we are able to acquire through them more information.

To slip through unobserved we need few people; for the smaller the parties are the quicker they will march, and get over difficult parts of the roads. A small squad discloses itself suddenly, and its safety lies in the amazement which its unexpected appearance will cause to the enemy, who will lose some moments in making up his mind to attack it. As long as an exploring patrol displays the necessary alertness, there will be little to fear, for its mobility will enable it to escape being overcome. In exploring, we incur the risk of having some parties cut off and captured; our losses will be less if we launch forth only small bodies.

Within a certain just limit we must economize our forces, relying more on artifice and skill than in numbers. In exploring we should endeavour to make up for the latter by the good quality of the elements, attaching more importance to the intelligent capacity of the soldiers, and to the condition of their horses, than to the exact strength of the party. A very small party of men is constrained to adhere to its *rôle* of exploring, for no other reason that it has not the temptation to measure its strength with the enemy. On the other hand, an officer who has the means is more prone to yield to temptation and get involved in a fight.

Brave men must overcome their horror of

turning their back on the foe, when this action is imposed on them by the nature of their duty. The obtaining of prompt and certain information is the object to be kept constantly in view; in doing this, prudence is more valuable than reckless bravery.

The habit of galloping back to report what other parties or an officer can see for themselves, which one frequently sees on field days, must be checked; for, acting in this manner, the trooper turns his back on the enemy and ceases to keep, as he should, his eyes constantly riveted on him. The dust and the glitter of arms is sure to draw the adversary's attention, whereas the leading principle in scouting is to conceal one's presence and to strive to watch without being seen.* Galloping along hard roads, rutty lanes, and across heavy ploughed fields may convey an idea of smartness to the uninitiated; in a campaign such a practice would soon knock up the horses, and those of an enterprising cavalry will have sufficient hard work to do without it. It is more in the field than at home that a trooper will have to

* In scouting at field days and manœuvres our horsemen do many things which it would be utterly impossible for them to do in war. We often see them careless in concealing their movements, lingering in dangerously exposed positions, pushing forward and mingling with the adversary's troops. All this is contrary to a true representation of war; consequently great attention should be paid in correcting such glaring faults when they occur.

husband the strength of his horse, for, when the opposing armies come into actual contact, the cavalry divisions will have to take part in the battle and in the pursuit. This they will never be able to do with horses which are worn out.

The cavalry must come face to face with the enemy in the best possible condition. Sobieski enjoins the greatest nursing of the horses. "Only the most constant vigilance of the officers and the incessant care of the troopers" (he says) "can preserve the cavalry from absolute ruin before it arrives on the battle-field."

What ruins the horses in war is fatigue. When a cavalry is enterprising, the utmost care is impotent to prevent fatigue; nevertheless, a thoughtful soldier must strive to do his best, by attentive nourishing and rest, to maintain the forces of his faithful companion.

In all that relates to information in the field all ranks should know, first, all the means which may be employed to acquire it; secondly, what particulars require to be communicated, and in what manner; thirdly, the officer to whom these should be detailed; fourthly, how the reports can be transmitted with speed and with every prospect of their reaching their intended destination.

The greater portion of the information which the cavalry will acquire will be the result of personal observation. This is but natural, considering that it is pushed forward to watch, to submit the enemy to an unremitting and diligent scrutiny, to spy out all his doings, and to take timely cognizance of all relevant indications. The information which it must seek is, however, not limited to what it can see for itself, but comprises also all what it can gather from the statements of other parties. Every care, nevertheless, must be taken to verify all current reports, always bearing in mind that "they say" is a great liar. The scouts having to keep the enemy constantly in sight, and to conform with all his movements, cannot linger to attend to this; they are, however, followed by larger bodies of men, who can undertake to question the inhabitants, making them reveal all they know of the whereabouts, number, movements, and habits of the foe. Something useful can also be extracted from prisoners and deserters.

Possibly not much time can be spared in making a searching examination of the latter, nevertheless, before sending them under escort to the rear, every endeavour should be made to get from them some insight into the actual state of affairs in the immediate front, being the direction from which they generally come.

On entering towns or villages which have been quitted quite recently by the enemy's forces, the inhabitants should be at once interrogated, and a summary of their statements passed to the rear. The manner in which the interrogation of the inhabitants, prisoners, and deserters should be conducted will form the subject of a subsequent chapter.

The documents, ordinances, notices, telegrams, newspapers, letters—in short, any printed or manuscript matter found in the enemy's country, may contain very valuable information; the cavalry must consequently be instructed to attach great importance to their seizure. Before the opening of the Jena campaign, on the 3rd of September, 1806, Napoleon instructed Marshal Berthier to solicit the King of Bavaria to have all the letters arriving at Augsberg and Nuremberg from Prussia seized and opened, to learn by their contents the opinion of the commercial world, and to discover any possible movements on the part of the Russians. Prussia, nevertheless, was not behindhand in her precautions; this is evident from the following passage found in a letter written by Bernadotte to Berthier: "I am told that the Berlin cabinet has ordered the director of the post to stop all letters directed to places which are occupied by the French army. It is doubtless owing to this measure that the opening of the mails at Nuremberg on the 16th instant has yielded no information. There were no letters amongst them coming from Berlin or Petersburg."

Addressing Murat from Auma, 12th of October, 1806, Napoleon writes: "Before noon to-day I will be at Gera. You will see, by the situation the army is in, that I completely envelop the enemy.

However, I need information of what he purposes doing. I hope you will find some in the post-office at Zeitz." One of the letters seized by Lieutenant von Horn at Ménil, on the 18th of August, 1870, was from the minister, Mons. de Chevreau, and informed the prefect that the Emperor of the French was at Chalons, where large numbers of troops were being concentrated.

The mails captured at Nancy in August, 1870, were sorted and translated by the agency of twenty one-year volunteers of the Rhein Dragoon Regiment, mostly young merchants' clerks from Frankfort. The information gleaned from the letters clearly indicated Metz and Chalons as the points on which the French forces were concentrating.

It is not sufficient to look in the post-offices and letter-boxes for any letters remaining there, but all found in public offices, hotels, private houses, etc., should be seized. In time of war, most of the correspondence, official as well as private, will contain something referring to the most absorbing topic of the day, and, when all these items are put together by an expert, they may reveal something which will interest the commander of the army. Individuals, in their simplicity, when writing about their family concerns, freely state what they have seen, without ever suspecting that often by this means they furnish the enemy with valuable information.

Orders, instructions, and memoranda must be

searched for on the belongings of the enemy's dead, of officers especially. Captain Ogilvy, an Irish adventurer, had been accredited as a representative of the Tours government with General Crouzat's army corps. He carried a letter from Mons. Gambetta, in which the war minister wrote: "Gein must be considered as the key of our position on the Loire." Ogilvy was killed at Ladon, and amongst his other papers was found Gambetta's letter, which was an important document for Prince Frederick Charles.

Very relevant items of information can be obtained by seizing the office copies of telegrams, and at times by tapping the enemy's wires. A bold dash round the enemy's flanks will enable an enterprising patrol to get at the enemy's side wires, and the rapidity with which mounted men can cover a certain distance makes this more possible when the adversary has concentrated his forces for battle. When instructions are issued to intercept the telegraphic communication of the enemy, telegraphists furnished with proper instruments will have to be attached to the cavalry. We should not count too much on this, for though an officer may have a fair knowledge of the enemy's language, the result of his superior education, this does not apply to an ordinary operator, who will be incompetent to read off a message sent in a strange language. We must also take into account that an alert enemy will not neglect to send all messages of a certain importance in cipher.

By appearing unexpectedly on a road which was considered safe, a party of cavalry may arrest couriers and intercept important orders or despatches, thus frustrating some intended combination of two forces. The non-arrival of an order at its destination, or a delay caused by having to make a considerable detour, for fear of falling in with the enemy's cavalry, may have important consequences in the operations. The absence of Bernadotte from the battle-field of Eylau and the consequent collapse of Napoleon's plans for hemming in the Russian army, was caused by the capture by a body of Cossacks of the staff officer who carried the emperor's instructions to the marshal. These cases will be rare now that the telegraph has become the ordinary means of communication in war; besides which the rule is to send orders and instructions by more than one courier and by different roads. The capture of the bearer may not always be rewarded by the seizure of the despatch, for he may have time to destroy it. De Brack recommends the barrel of a pistol as the best place for concealing a written message; if the bearer, on being pursued, sees no prospect of evading capture, by firing his pistol he can destroy it.

Should there be any possibility of the bearer having to destroy the message, the precaution should be taken to instruct him in what he should communicate to the officer he is sent to. By asking him to repeat several times what has been said, he will have it impressed on his mind, and the sender may feel more confident that he will repeat the message in the exact sense in which it was framed.

When a soldier sets too great a value on his intelligence, he is little disposed to hear what is being explained to him. "All right, enough; I fully understand," he may say before one has quite finished what one wishes to tell him. He hurries off without having taken the trouble to listen attentively, judging that he knows exactly what he has to report. This heedlessness often leads to unfortunate results, and when noticed must be reproved. The soldier must be trained to listen attentively, so as to convey a message as far as possible in the exact words in which it has been imparted to him.

There are certain minor details in scouting and exploring which should not be overlooked. Horses given to neighing or of a fretful disposition are unfitted for these duties. Every care should be taken to conceal bright ornaments which, by their glitter, may draw the enemy's attention. Clanking picketing chains, scabbard rings, etc., are objectionable, for they make a noise and are heard a long way off. When it is a question of surprising the enemy it is easy to preserve silence. Silence, nevertheless, is not all that is required, for there are other precautions to be taken to escape being detected when roving through the enemy's country. The lighting of fires, the striking of matches, the manner of challenging, the rules for unsaddling the horses, and the measures of security to be taken, are all particulars which demand attention. The regulations on all these points should be well known to all ranks, as the safety of a detachment or small part will greatly depend on their observation.

CHAPTER VI.

REPORTS AND THEIR TRANSMISSION.

All information acquired must be speedily reported to the officer principally concerned. This can be effected in two ways, by word of mouth and in writing. To send reports orally is a careless way of acting, for of three individuals who have a share in the communication, only one knows exactly how matters stand. Not only the bearer of the message may have failed to grasp its full meaning, but, through distraction or a faulty memory, he may omit to impart some very important particulars. Nor have we an absolute certainty that the officer who receives the message accepts it in the sense in which it was originally framed. In a verbal report there is the chance of its being forgotten, or of its significance being lost amongst the many which crowd on the mind; whereas in a written report we have the exact words of the sender, the document is ever present to be referred to whenever it is thought desirable, and the responsibility of both the sender and the receiver are fixed.

The vagueness which is often the worst feature of a verbal report does not exist when the statement is written down. *Viva voce* reports should be confined to information given direct by the observer to the individual concerned; but even in such cases, before the particulars are passed to the rear, they should be committed to writing. When the soldier who has acquired the news conveys it himself, we are not only able to learn exactly what he has seen, but by questioning we may elicit from him further details. As a rule written reports are only made by officers and superior non-commissioned officers.

Much can be communicated in a few words in the style of a telegram, and, when ordinary foresight is used, no one will be able to plead a want of writing materials. To meet this, officers and non-commissioned officers might be furnished with special note-books with perforated leaves and carbolic paper, by which means a number of reports can be sent, whilst the sender retains the duplicate of each of his messages.

Officers and non-commissioned officers who in the yearly manœuvres and other exercises, have been trained in sending written reports, will experience little difficulty in putting down the exact state of things in a few words. The habit of taking rough notes on the march should be encouraged, for it will help when having to send reports to the rear.

The leader of a cavalry exploring patrol must observe great care in the wording of a report, for it is on this that the officer commanding a cavalry division will decide on the most desirable measures to be taken.

As a rule an officer or a non-commissioned officer should abstain from transmitting any information the exactness of which he has not been able to verify in person. Should they, nevertheless, receive some very important revelation from a scout, from a patrol, or from any other source, they would be in fault to withhold it from the officer principally concerned until they have had time to convince themselves of its accuracy. The correct course to pursue, if the information is of sufficient gravity, is to pass it at once to the rear, then to try by all means to ascertain the truth and send a second report.

A report may contain some particulars which are positive, some which are current, and some which are only a surmise. The communication should always clearly distinguish between the things the writer has seen with his own eyes, and what he has learnt from others. In the latter case the source of such information should be given, stating if it has been corroborated or not by the testimony of others. Though the writer may have good grounds for doubting the accuracy of any hearsay information, he should give it all the same, adding the reasons which lead him to believe that it is improbable. Very unexpected things often occur in war, and this should make us careful not to suppress any particulars for the simple reason that they appear to us unlikely to be true.

The indispensable qualities of a report are simplicity, exactness, legibility, and accuracy with regard to time,* or the spelling of names of localities and individuals. All ambiguous expression such as to the right, to the left, to the front, to the rear, should be very carefully avoided; all indications as to the direction should be given with reference to the points of the compass. The banks of streams and rivers should be described as the right or the left bank.

It is of greater consequence to detail accurately the most relevant points than to waste time in describing the more insignificant particulars. The writer must confine himself to furnish precise information regarding the enemy. He should show where he is and what has been seen of him, the different arms his forces are composed of, the number and designation of the various regiments, their approximate strength, and such points as relate to the situation of his camps or bivouacs, his manner of guarding himself, the direction of his march or the strength of the position he occupies.

In describing the enemy's troops, it is seemly to give the colour of their uniforms and of their facings,

* To secure uniformity of time throughout, the watches on service must be regulated on a standard timekeeper.

to detail any peculiarity in their head-dress and the like; such particulars will convey a good indication of the units to which they belong.

Whilst giving a brief and clear account of what has been seen or of what has come to notice, an officer or a non-commissioned officer should abstain from giving a very decided opinion. The horizon of any single detachment is very small, and such an opinion can only be formed where the information coming from different sources focuses; there alone can a proper degree of importance be assigned to each separate report.

When a report is to announce that a party is compelled to fall back, it should clearly show before what troops the retreat is effected.

It is a commendable precaution to note on the report the names of some of the men who were with the sender at the time, thus, in the event of his being subsequently captured or killed, there will be others who can be questioned and give the information in his stead.

Those rendered by superior officers should indicate the steps which have been taken to meet any extraordinary display of enterprise on the part of the enemy, or to defeat any vigorous measures which he may have adopted to strew difficulties in the way of our exploration. Acting in this manner there will be no necessity for the general commanding to issue orders for meeting the difficulties which the cavalry divisions may have to contend against.

The dispositions have already been taken by an officer who, being on the spot, is best able to take in the situation and to judge which is the proper course to pursue.

Some writers, with good reason, insist on the necessity for furnishing a report at certain stated hours, if nothing more, in the early morning and in the evening. The great care which should be taken in sparing any unnecessary fatigue to both men and horses must never be carried to excess. The absence of any report whatsoever from a certain direction is liable to cause uneasiness, and might give rise to all manner of unfavourable suppositions; their rendering, therefore, should not be left to option, but should be laid down as a general regulation.

Even when there is nothing particular to relate, a brief report should be furnished, for it cannot but ease the general's mind to know that in a given district the cavalry has found no trace of the enemy, and that he has nothing to fear in that direction. If the report contains nothing absolutely new, it may nevertheless tend to confirm what has already been ascertained from other sources. A report in writing, on the other hand, is imperative whenever there is something of consequence to communicate, and then it should be despatched as speedily as possible. All that has been ascertained concerning the enemy must then form the subject of a special communication.

The one sent in the evening should recapitulate

what has been seen or gathered from any source during the day. When this is despatched about sundown, it may reach army headquarters before the arrangements for the morrow's movements have been quite completed.

In the morning the report should state what the enemy has been about during the night, what alterations in his position have been noticed, if there was any movement on foot amongst his forces, at what hour and in which direction, if his outposts have been reinforced.

In a report it is always necessary to indicate the distances; this shows the importance which should always attach to judging distances by the eye. However inaccurate this method may be, still, being the most expeditious, it will be found to answer most purposes. Schellendorf* gives the following particulars. "With good eyesight, on an ordinary clear day, it is generally admitted that the following objects should be distinguished on the sky-line—

"At a distance of 15 to 20 kilometres,† church spires and towns.

"At a distance of 8 to 12 kilometres, windmills.

"At a distance of 3 to 4 kilometres, chimneys of a light colour.

* Bronsart von Schellendorf, "The Duties of the General Staff," vol. i. p. 264.

† A kilometre is equal to five-eighths of an English mile.

"At a distance of 2 kilometres, trunks of large trees.

"At a distance of 1 kilometre, single posts.

"At 500 metres, the panes of glass may be distinguished in a window, and at from 200 to 250 metres the tiles of a roof or of a building."

The location of cities, towns, and villages can be exactly fixed by the appearance of one spire or church tower, or by the clouds of smoke which, when the air is still, hang about them. To ascertain from a distance whether any one is occupied by the enemy, the place must be watched long and at different times of the day. Sentries will be probably observed posted on some points, also an unusual number of men in the streets will give some indication. It should be carefully noted if at any time during the day the horses are brought out to be watered, and whether trains or convoys of wagons moving into the place stop there or simply pass through.

Not only has the information to be acquired, but it must be communicated as quickly as possible. Things are liable to undergo considerable modification in such a brief period of time, that a particular which was exact at a given instant may in an hour become false and useless. It is obvious that if a commander, not to let a favourable opportunity escape him, has to take his measures and issue his orders on the receipt of very important news, this must reach him with all possible speed.

Other reports may follow in corroboration of the first, but the first must be sent to him with the utmost despatch.

The acquisition of information is only the first part of the task which the cavalry or a reconnoitring officer will have to undertake; the second, and, generally speaking, by far the most difficult, is to let it reach as speedily as possible the commander who is anxiously waiting to receive it. The information itself is not naturally of the same consequence to the individual who acquires it as it is to the general who is far in rear; its value, therefore, will always increase with the speed with which it is placed in his hands.

In a country in which the population is violent and undaunted it will be imprudent to send information to the rear by a single trooper; it may often be expedient for the entire patrol to regain the supports with the intelligence acquired.

Naturally what is furnished by the reconnoitring parties belonging to the cavalry divisions must in the first instance be sent to the officer commanding each division, for his movements are dependent on what is discovered by his advanced parties. It is this officer who has to keep the commander-in-chief informed of the movements and dispositions of the enemy, the information he furnishes in his turn must consequently be a summary of what has been gathered by the reconnoitring parties which precede the march of his division.

Though all reports coming from the front should go direct to him, this will not preclude their purport being communicated to the commanders of any bodies of troops the bearers may meet on the road. With regard to the general situation, it will rest with the divisional commander to consider what particulars out of the reports that reach him he should communicate to the commander of the nearest army corps.

The manner in which the connection between the cavalry divisions and the headquarters of the army is kept up requires to be carefully studied. It is not sufficient to declare in a general and vague manner that it is always of great moment to maintain a constant relation between the various portions of an army; what is required is to lay down in a very positive way the most practical system for keeping up this intercommunication. If in the yearly manœuvres we devote special attention to the most expeditious means for transmitting information to places far in the rear under a variety of circumstances, we shall not leave the matter on service to the initiative of officers who may have a limited experience of the obstacles and delays which so very frequently occur in this particular point in war. Some experiments in this way appear to us to be very much needed, as the subject has never been sufficiently thought out. When the manner of operating has been submitted to a very practical test, it will be possible to frame valuable instructions on this duty for the guidance of all concerned.

It is not to be expected that the cavalry divisions will be able to make any use of the telegraph for this purpose, for the enemy in retiring will certainly close the telegraph stations and sever the communication. In default of the electric telegraph they might fall back on visual signalling; but the establishment of a good chain of stations—especially in a flat and wooded country—can hardly keep pace with the cavalry advance. The heliograph, the most portable and far-reaching instrument, requires sunshine, which may not be at our command at a critical moment. Ordinarily, therefore, the cavalry will have nothing else to rely on but its own men, selecting always such as are mounted on the swiftest horses.

In the general movement, effectual measures must be taken to provide against the bearers of reports wandering about a strange country, wasting valuable time in seeking for the main body, whose whereabouts cannot but be more or less uncertain. The commander who sends out the reconnoitring parties should attend to this; knowing the direction which they have taken, he should have no difficulty in indicating some locality in their rear for which the troopers bearing messages should be directed to make in the first instance. This rendezvous—which when possible should be in the neighbourhood of some conspicuous landmark—must be occupied by a strong detachment under command of an officer.

The following is given as an instance of a detachment which went astray from the want of some such precaution:—*

"The 1st squadron of the 10th Hussars, which had been sent (on the 13th of August) in the direction of Nancy, sends back two platoons from Nancy to Château-Salins, to escort treasure and forage requisitioned on the previous day. One of the platoons returns to Nancy to serve a fresh requisition.

"The troopers who had been despatched in the night to report to the general commanding the 5th division return without having been able to find the division. An officer is then sent, who receives orders to report directly to the staff of the Xth Corps.

* * * * *

"The squadron of the 10th Hussars sent towards Nancy is lost to the regiment until the 16th of September. The officer who conveyed to the Xth Corps a report of the operations of this squadron returned without orders, without indications. The captain then addresses himself to the staff of the 4th Cavalry Division, which had then arrived at Nancy; he is given a vague direction to the N.W., on the strength of which he goes wandering about for more than a month in search of his regiment."

What has been said above is, after all, only the

* *Revue de Cavalerie*, Avril 1895, "Opérations de la 5e Division De Cavalerie Allemande du 12 au 15 Aout, 1870."

first step in the transmission of reports; arrangements must be made for their speedy conveyance to the headquarters of the general commanding, which, under ordinary circumstances, will be many miles in rear. The best and usual system is to divide this distance into stages of moderate length, and whilst advancing to drop a small squad of men at the end of each one. Though these posts should be established in such a manner as to insure all possible rapidity in the transmission of information and orders, we must guard from having too many, on account of the number of cavalry soldiers they withdraw from other duties. The points to consider therefore are, the most advantageous intervals between these posts—so as to spare the horses as much as practicable—and the number of men each one should consist of.

No hard and fast rules can be laid down as to the first point, for the nature of the country and the disposition of the population must have always a certain influence in determining the length of each stage. If the country is hilly, if the roads lead through many woods, hollows and defiles, if the people are hostile, the posts will naturally have to be placed closer to each other than would be necessary under dissimilar conditions.

The time occupied by horses in covering a certain distance might afford a better guide. This, however, demands discrimination, for all that relates to pace seems to be based on what obtains in ordinary times, when the troopers travel on good roads, in fair weather, and are free from any pre-occupation. In war, having to keep an incessant look out, and the mind being tormented by the possibility of being intercepted, cannot but have a retarding influence on the pace. If we base our calculations on a medium rate of speed we shall not be far out; if the horses do the distance in less time it will be so much gained, whereas, by fixing on a maximum, we incur the risk of being disappointed in our expectations. General Lewal, who has examined this question in his "Tactique des Renseignements," comes to the following conclusions. Average per hour, trot and walk, alternately, 10 kilometres (6$\frac{2}{8}$ miles); trot alone, 15 kilometres (9$\frac{3}{8}$ miles); gallop, 20 kilometres (12$\frac{1}{2}$ miles). In war he considers that for trot and walk alternately, we should count on 8 kilometres (5 miles); for trot alone, 11 kilometres (6$\frac{7}{8}$ miles); for gallop, 15 kilometres (9$\frac{3}{8}$ miles). He quotes an order issued by Napoleon in 1812, in which the emperor demanded a uniform speed of two leagues, about eight kilometres, per hour, and three cases taken from the performances of the German cavalry in their last war, in which the speed attained throughout amounted to about as much.

It is vain to indicate an average for these stages, for their establishment must always depend on the actual conditions of the country, which can only come to our knowledge at the time.

On the point of the number of men to be assigned to each post, General Bronsart von Schellendorf recommends one non-commissioned officer and six men; Perizonius and Colonel de Savoye, one non-commissioned officer and from three to nine men. Much must naturally depend on the amount of cavalry available; with small posts there is always a greater liability of the men being captured. When the men can be spared, there is an advantage in having nine men—as Colonel de Savoye points out—inasmuch as the party can be divided into three watches, one-third to be always ready to mount with a sentry on the look out, the other two-thirds can unbridle, and, if it is considered safe, half of the latter can even unsaddle. A less numerous post has hardly the men sufficient to carry on the work in both directions, particularly at night, when it is always prudent to send the men in couples, not merely to afford each other mutual confidence, but to make head against any unforeseen accident.

Everything should be done to save work to the troop horses and to curtail as much as practicable the number of cavalry men employed on this duty. It will often be possible to secure, on requisition, light and well-horsed two-wheeled vehicles for the express purpose of transmitting reports. In such cases the infantry can replace the cavalry in many stages, and the work can be conducted with nearly the same rapidity.

Amongst the many novelties which have become

very popular in recent years is the cycle, and its application to military purposes has introduced a new element in the speedy transmission of information in war. Leaving on one side the question of employing cyclists as scouts, or of turning cycles into means of transport for mobile infantry, there cannot be any doubt that cyclists can render important services if employed as despatch-bearers, and as means of communication between the advance-posts and the main body in rear. This was the original conception; however, we find that when in their manœuvres of 1875 the Italians, for the first time, tested the employment of bicycles, the riders principally conveyed the correspondence between the battalion commanders and the chief of the supply service.

Cyclists can go wherever cavalry can, and can not only keep pace with its movements, but in the long run are able to outstrip the very best horse. They can consequently relieve the troopers and horses from endless fatigue in carrying messages and reports. Thus, by reducing the pure courier work, they would keep the horsemen more together, limiting the number of relay parties to be echelonned on the roads. In cycling there is no animal to feed, groom, and look after; there is no animal liable to become disabled; and, whereas the sound of a horse moving at speed—above all in a still night—is heard a long way off, the cyclist progresses at a rapid pace without making any noise.

Cyclists can travel long distances without relays, and at the end of a long run are not borne down by fatigue. A man on horseback presents a large target, not so a man on a bicycle; certainly the former can make use of his weapons if attacked, this a cyclist cannot do, and he must simply trust to his speed. If a road is considered unsafe they can nevertheless move in couples, and the precaution can always be taken of sending other parties by different roads.

The expertness in reading a map which they acquire in the pursuit of their exercise makes cyclists very adapted for moving through a strange country. It will be objected that they require good roads and not a too hilly country, but many provincial roads and country lanes in dry weather are fairly suited for the purpose. Given, however, that a cyclist, for any reason whatsoever, cannot follow the most direct road, he can make a detour, and his speed will enable him to reach his destination in very good time. The average speed per hour which can be calculated on in day time ranges from nine to thirteen miles; at night it is much less, and seldom exceeds six miles—on a known road it will be something more. A speed of thirteen miles per hour, kept up for several consecutive hours, is a good pace for maintaining communication between the fractions of an outpost force, or between the advance-posts and the main body. We should reflect that whatever may be the speed of horses, at every relay there must occur a loss of time, from the despatch having to change hands, having to be registered and receipted. Not so with cyclists, for they can travel from end to end. The speed of horses is also much reduced, and the chances of a fall are augmented, when the roads are made slippery from frost; but this does not present quite the same impediment to a cyclist.

The records of long rides which have been performed by well-trained cyclists are well known, but what is to our purpose is to see if their speed and freedom of going can be turned to account in war. What we mainly advocate is the substitution of cyclists for troopers in the duty of transmitting reports and conveying orders, for every one admits how ruinous this service is to the horses. In the field they lose condition and break down through hard work, exposure, and irregular feeding, and, if they can be relieved from much travelling backward and forward on hard roads, it will be so much gained when the time comes for the cavalry to measure its strength with the enemy.

The best field for cyclists is the zone between the independent cavalry divisions and the head of the heavy columns, where the roads have not yet been cut up by the passage of artillery and heavy wagons.

Lightning Source UK Ltd.
Milton Keynes UK
UKOW05f2230120716
278239UK00005B/122/P